All Things in Balance

by Tamara Jasmine Burrell

Glenview, Illinois • Boston, Massachusetts • Chandler, Arizona
Upper Saddle River, New Jersey

Herbivores

grass

Thompson's gazelle

Thompson's gazelles live in Africa.

The balance of nature is important. When nature is balanced, living things grow. They eat well. They live well. They also need each other to live.

Some animals eat only plants. They are called herbivores. Sometimes they are called plant-eaters. These animals eat leaves and roots. They also eat seeds and nuts. Some eat fruits and grass.

Some herbivores live in Africa. Gazelles and elephants are both herbivores.

Carnivores

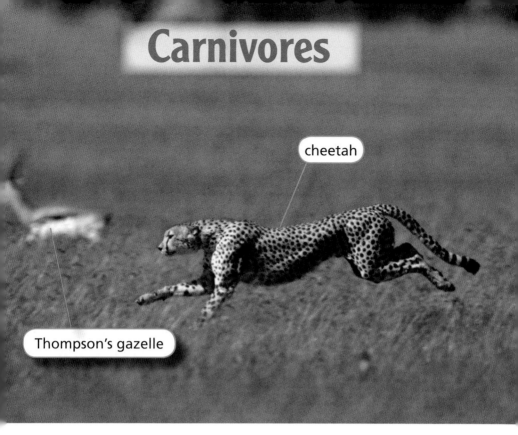

cheetah

Thompson's gazelle

Cheetahs hunt herbivores.

Some animals eat other animals. They are called carnivores. Sometimes they are called meat-eaters or predators.

Big cats in Africa are carnivores. A cheetah is one of these big cats. Cheetahs like to eat Thompson's gazelles. The gazelles can run about 50 miles an hour. Cheetahs can run up to 70 miles an hour. Cheetahs cannot run fast for long, though. After 20 seconds, a cheetah must stop. It gets too hot. Then the gazelle can get away.

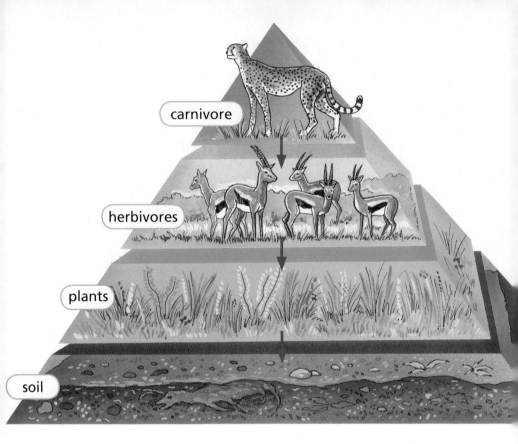

carnivore

herbivores

plants

soil

Food Chains

All living things need food. Most plants get food from water and sunshine. They also get nutrients from the dirt. All living things need nutrients to live and grow.

Herbivores eat plants. Then carnivores eat herbivores. Carnivores also sometimes eat other carnivores. Living things become food for other living things. This is called the food chain.

At the top of the chain, there are fewer living things. There are many things at the bottom. Things on the top eat things on the bottom.

Nature in Balance

The balance of nature works well. Carnivores eat some herbivores. Other herbivores stay alive. Herbivores eat some of the plants. The plants have dirt and water to grow. Most living things stay healthy.

Nature Out of Balance

Sometimes there are too many herbivores. Then there is not enough food for them. Some of them die. Then there is less food for the carnivores. Soon the carnivores die too.

There are no animals to eat the plants. Too many plants grow. They fight for water and sunshine. They fight for nutrients in the dirt. Then the plants begin to die too. Nature is out of balance.

What Upsets the Balance?

One kind of fox lives in California. It eats birds and small animals. It also eats fruit. It is called an omnivore. Omnivores eat both plants and animals.

Long ago, no carnivores ate the foxes. Then people brought pigs to where the foxes live. Some of the pigs became wild.

Then eagles came. They came to eat the wild pigs. Now the eagles eat the foxes too. Today, the foxes are endangered. This means they could die out forever.

People learned that some changes are bad. They can upset the balance of nature. So now people are working hard. They want to bring the balance back.

Glossary

bal•ance of na•ture
(bal ′əns of nā ′cher), *NOUN*. the right number of plants and animals in a place

car•ni•vore
(kär ′nə vôr), *NOUN*. a meat-eating animal; predator

en•dan•gered
(en dān ′jerd) *ADJECTIVE*. in danger of dying out forever

food chain
(füd chān), *NOUN*. the order in which living things become food for other things

her•bi•vore
(ėr ′bə vôr), *NOUN*. a plant-eating animal

om•ni•vore
(om ′nə vôr ′), *NOUN*. an animal that eats both plants and animals

---

Extend Language   Latin Word Parts

Some words in English come from other languages. Parts of these words come from the Latin language:

Carni- in the word *carnivore* means "meat."

Herbi- in the word *herbivore* means "kinds of plants."

Omni- in the word *omnivore* means "all."